Following Aslan

A Book of Devotions for Children

Anamchara Books

Vestal, NY 13850
www.anamcharabooks.com

Copyright © 2006 Anamchara Books

All rights reserved. No part of this book may be reproduced or trans-mitted in any form or by any means electronic or mechanical includ-ing photocopying and recording, or by any information storage and retrieval system, without permission in writing by the publisher.

Produced by Harding House Publishing Service, Inc.,
Vestal, New York.

Cover art by Evangeline Ehl.
Illustrations, cover design, and interior design by MK Bassett-Harvey.

ISBN (*Ingram paperback edition*): 978-1-62524-880-0

Unless otherwise noted, all Bible quotations are from the *Holy Bible, New International Version®*.
Copyright © 1973, 1978, 1984 International Bible Society. Used by permission of Zondervan. All rights reserved.

Following Aslan

A Book of Devotions for Children

based upon
The Chronicles of Narnia by C.S. Lewis

by Kenneth R. McIntosh, M.Div.

A Note to Parents

At the end of *Voyage of the Dawn Treader*, the third of C. S. Lewis's fantasy novels about the land of Narnia, the children regret they must leave the marvelous Lion Aslan and return to their own country. Aslan assures them he will meet them again in England: "But there I have another name. You must learn to know me by that name. That was the very reason you were brought to Narnia, that by knowing me here for a little, you may know me better there."

That is the purpose of this book: to suggest the connections between Aslan and his identity in our world—Jesus Christ. This is a devotional book for children, designed to help them interact with God via the creative ideas and images in C. S. Lewis's wonderful series of books, *The Chronicles of Narnia*. C. S. Lewis was a devout Christian, and forty years after Lewis's death, his books of theology such as *Mere Christianity* are still major sellers. His in-depth and creative thinking about Christianity continues to shape our world.

Following Aslan

Following Aslan is written simply enough that children should be capable of reading the book on their own, but I hope many children and parents will read the book together, perhaps as a nightly custom. This book contains an ample amount of theology, and thoughts about God are often deep and difficult. Theology sometimes gets a bad rap: people say they want to *experience* God rather than study *about* him—but at the same time, we cannot help but try to figure out God. Even young children—sometimes, *especially* young children—have plenty of ideas and questions about who God is and how they should relate to him. This book acts as a guide for that thinking and questioning process, helping children to see God's relevance to their own everyday lives.

Of course, different churches and individual believers hold a wide variety of theologies. In this book, I have tried to communicate the beliefs held by C. S. Lewis as best I understand him through his other writings. You may or may not agree with him on all points. Thus, reading this book and talking with your children as you do so gives you the opportunity to teach, correct, and dialogue with your children regarding your own spiritual beliefs.

Likewise, the Narnia stories communicate a number of important life lessons. Unfortunately, our world is more dangerous than Edwardian England was, so I have updated some of these ideas, making them pertinent to today's world. Again, it is important to interact with your son or daughter about

A Note to Parents

these matters; you are their primary guide to life in this complex and challenging world.

Finally, this book is a conversation between art and truth; *The Chronicles of Narnia* are imaginative creations, and from them we seek deeper insight into the truths of our world. My insights may differ from your insights into Mr. Lewis's fantasy world, and your child may have an entirely different set of ideas about the stories. Sometimes, children's insights are the best of all! Of course, recognizing the allegory in Lewis's fiction should in no way detract from its richness as great children's literature. Hopefully, by drawing out the allegorical meanings coded in the Narnia books we shall gain even greater respect for the books as works of art.

So consider this book an invitation to a lively dialogue between Mr. C. S. Lewis, yourself, your children, and God. I hope we will all grow wiser and better as a result.

Sincerely, Ken McIntosh

Meeting the King

Imagine what it would be like if you were to meet someone very special, such as the president of the United States, or your favorite actor or music star. Would you be nervous?

In *The Lion, the Witch and the Wardrobe*, Peter, Susan, and Lucy are nervous when they meet the great king, Aslan. The children have heard about Aslan from their friends, Mr. and Mrs. Beaver, who told them Aslan is a lion—in fact, he is the great lion. Susan admits she is afraid and asks if Aslan is a "safe" lion. Mr. Beaver tells her that Aslan is not safe, "but he's good."

Meeting the King

When they do meet Aslan, the children discover the lion king is "good and terrible at the same time." However, after meeting him, they discover that Aslan knows their names, knows all their troubles, and cares about them even though they have done some bad things. All three children feel "glad and quiet" just standing in front of Aslan.

The Lion, the Witch and the Wardrobe is a wonderful story, with brave children, great adventures, and magical characters. At the same time, it explains the spiritual reality that is all around us today. The man who wrote the Narnia stories was an Englishman named Clive Staples Lewis, a very smart man, a teacher at a famous college whose life changed when he met Jesus Christ. The Bible calls Jesus "the Lion of the Tribe of Judah," and in Mr. Lewis's Narnia stories, Aslan stands for Jesus Christ.

You can meet Jesus, and you do not have to go through a magical wardrobe to do so. You probably will not see Jesus with your eyes (very few people do that), but you can talk with him, nonetheless. Jesus said in the Bible, "And be sure of this, I am with you always" (Matthew 28:20).

How does it feel to talk with Jesus, the King? Well, it feels much the same way as the children felt when they met Aslan. The Bible says when we meet Jesus, we "rejoice with trembling" (Psalm 2:11). Like Aslan, Jesus is both great and caring—and yet we are just a little bit afraid of him, because he is so great. After all, the Bible says Jesus made the stars, the sun, our Planet Earth, and he made you and me. At the same

Following Aslan

time, we are happy to meet him, and our fear melts away as we realize how much he loves us. He wants to be your friend, a friend who will be with you every moment of your life. He already knows the unkind things you have done (and will do in the future), yet he likes you anyway, and he still wants very much to be with you.

Here is a prayer you can say when you meet with Jesus, the Great King:

> *Jesus, I am a little afraid because I see how awesome you are and how small I am in front of you. But I know that you already love me and want to be my best friend, even though you are a great king. Help me to be a good friend to you and follow you always.*

The Invisible World

At the start of *The Lion, the Witch and the Wardrobe*, the four children are excited to explore the big old house where they have gone to live with the Professor. Lucy goes into the wardrobe and walks through it into another world, the magical

Following Aslan

realm called Narnia. She meets a faun (a man with goat legs), Mr. Tumnus, and then returns to England. Later, when she tries to tell her brothers and sisters about Narnia, they think she is crazy.

Peter and Susan talk with the Professor about Lucy: Is she out of her mind, claiming there is another world next to ours? The Professor surprises Susan and Peter with his reply; he believes Lucy is telling the truth. When Peter asks the Professor if he really believes "that there could be other worlds—all over the place, just around the corner—like that?" the Professor tells him, "Nothing is more probable."

The Bible tells us that there is indeed another world, very close to our own, yet invisible. God and the angels live in this near but invisible world. Some adults make fun of this idea, just as Lucy's brothers and sister did. People like this say, "If you cannot see it, it does not exist." Is that true? Do invisible things not exist? Think about television and radio waves: your TV and radio receive invisible waves that bring music and shows to your home. Although you do not see or feel these invisible waves, they are still real, and you would miss them if they didn't exist. In the same way, there is an invisible world near to our own.

C. S. Lewis, who wrote *The Lion, the Witch and the Wardrobe*, was a very smart man. Besides his Narnia stories, he wrote books for adults that scientists and other highly educated people read. Mr. Lewis believed an invisible world exists right beside our own world, one we cannot ordinarily see, and some

The Invisible World

brilliant scientists today agree with him. They speak of "parallel universes," big words that mean, as the Professor says, "other worlds . . . just around the corner."

Once in a while, people in our world get a glimpse of the invisible world. When this happens, we call it a miracle. However, we can speak to this invisible world all the time: prayer is like your own private telephone line to Narnia. Like Lucy, you have friends in the world next door. The Bible says, "If you make the Lord your refuge, if you make the Most High your shelter, no evil will conquer you. . . . For he orders his angels to protect you wherever you go" (Psalm 91:9,11).

Here is a prayer you can say, speaking to God in the invisible world:

> *God, I do not see you, your Son, or your angels, but I know they exist. I believe you are near me, like the radio waves that I cannot see but that are around me all the time. I know you see me, even when I do not see you; I know you protect me and watch over me, so I can rely on you and not be afraid of the things I do see. Thank you for your angels and your invisible hand of protection.*

Sons of Adam, Daughters of Eve

When Lucy first enters the land of Narnia, Mr. Tumnus asks her, "Should I be right in thinking that you are a Daughter of Eve?" In all the Narnia books, the residents of Narnia call the children "Sons of Adam and Daughters of Eve"—a reminder that all the people who live on Earth share the same two human parents.

You probably don't go around thinking of yourself as a "Daughter of Eve" or "Son of Adam," but if you did, you might realize how much all people are alike. You can look at your mom and dad and think how you resemble them: perhaps you have your mom's hair color or your dad's nose, or maybe you say things in a way that makes people remark, "You sound just like your mother!" In the same way, Mr. Lewis in his books reminds us that we are all somewhat like our great, great, great, great (and on-and-on-great) grandparents Adam and Eve.

There are good and bad things about that. As Aslan says in the second Narnia book, *Prince Caspian*, "You come of the Lord Adam and the Lady Eve. . . . And that is both honour enough to erect the head of the poorest beggar and shame enough to bow the shoulders of the greatest emperor on earth."

It is a great honor to be a Son of Adam or Daughter of Eve, because the Bible says the Lord made all of us "in the image of God" (Genesis 1:27). Like God the Creator, we are creative! You can probably draw, sing, or make some impressive things out of Legos®—your special talents are like God's own creative nature. The way you treat others can also be like God: when you feel bad because someone else is hurting, or when you share your favorite toy or game with someone else, you show you are made in God's image.

Following Aslan

At the same time, as Aslan says, we share shame as the Sons of Adam and the Daughters of Eve. The third chapter of Genesis in the Bible tells how our first parents failed to love God and do what he told them. Because of their disobedience, many sad things happened: Adam and Eve hurt each other and began to mess up our wonderful planet, all because they turned away from God.

That is why Jesus came into the world, so human beings could become more like God. Jesus is like a bridge we can walk across so we can be close to God—and once we are close to him, he can help us become more like him. Jesus washes away the shame of being a Daughter of Eve or Son of Adam.

Here is a prayer about being Sons of Adam and Daughters of Eve:

God, I thank you for making my first parents, Adam and Eve, and for making me like them. Thank you that I can be like you—creative and caring. Help me to love all other people and all the creatures you made on this earth. At the same time, I know I can be like Adam and Eve in their shame—selfish and hurtful. When I do that, please forgive me for Jesus's sake, and help me to get close to you.

A Change of Heart

In *The Lion, the Witch and Wardrobe*, Mr. Tumnus at first acts very nicely toward Lucy. He shares his umbrella with her, invites her to his cave, and prepares a little snack for her. Unlike Lucy, you probably already know *you should never, ever for any reason go anywhere with a stranger!* If someone invites you to come to his or her car for candy or offers to give you a toy for no reason, you should run right to your parents and tell them. Although there are many good people in the world, there are also people who might hurt you. In fact, Mr. Tumnus was acting so nice for a reason—he meant to kidnap Lucy and take her to the White Witch!

Fortunately for Lucy, Mr. Tumnus has a change of heart. He begins crying and confesses to being a bad faun. When Lucy tries to comfort him, he tells her of his evil plan to kidnap her. He is afraid of the bad things the White Witch might do to him if she finds out he let a human go; she might even turn him to stone! Yet Mr. Tumnus makes a brave choice: he turns away from the evil he was planning and instead helps Lucy escape back to her own world.

The Bible talks a lot about people changing their mind from bad to good. For example, when God sent a man named John to get people ready to meet Jesus, John told everyone, "Stop doing bad things and do good instead . . . if you have two coats and someone is cold, give her your jacket. . . . Don't cheat people or make money dishonestly." (See Luke 3:7–14.)

No one is perfect, and sooner or later you will probably do something you know is wrong. When you do, you'll feel guilty and wonder how to get rid of that awful feeling. That is like Mr. Tumnus, when he felt bad about turning Lucy over to the White Witch. Like Mr. Tumnus, you can change direction.

One reason you feel bad when you do wrong is that you are hiding something—from your parents or your friends or your teacher. If you are keeping something secret, it probably means you shouldn't have done it in the first place, and now you are afraid to tell anyone. However, you will feel better if you

A Change of Heart

admit what you have done instead of hide it. If you confess something, you might get punished: perhaps you'll be sent to your room, or you might have to apologize to someone you hurt. You'll probably feel embarrassed. But you'll also find a way to do what's right, and then you'll no longer have that bad feeling.

When you do something wrong, change direction. It might be embarrassing, and you might get punished, but you will feel better later for doing the right thing.

Here is a prayer for when you have a change of heart, turning in a good direction:

God, thank you for loving me even when I make bad choices. You know everything I do: so give me courage like Mr. Tumnus, to choose to do the right thing even if it is difficult and I might be punished or have to apologize. Thank you, God, that I can always turn in the right direction, and you will always continue to love me.

Turkish Delight

When Edmund meets the White Witch in *The Lion, the Witch and the Wardrobe*, she asks him if he would like something to eat. He says, "Turkish Delight." She produces magical candies, enchanted so that "anyone who had once tasted it would want more and more of it, and would even, if they were allowed, go on eating it till they killed themselves."

Turkish Delight

The first time I read the book, I wondered, "What is Turkish Delight?" Since then I have learned that it is a soft, sticky candy coated with sugar (somewhat like gumdrops). Here is a recipe for Turkish Delight you could make with your parents. (Don't worry, this isn't enchanted Turkish Delight!)

Ingredients:

2 cups granulated sugar
1 1/4 cups water
1 lemon, the peel cut into strips, the juice squeezed and strained
1 orange, the peel cut into strips, the juice squeezed and strained
4 tablespoons unflavored powdered gelatin
2 tablespoons confectioners' sugar
1 tablespoon cornstarch

What to do:

Dissolve the granulated sugar in half of the water over medium heat.
Add the strips of lemon and orange peel, the rest of the water, and the juices.
Bring the mixture to a boil and simmer for 15 minutes.
Soak the gelatin in the mixture for 5 to 10 minutes.

Following Aslan

Strain the mixture into a shallow, dampened pan or onto platters, and let it set for 24 hours.
Cut the candy into 1-inch squares.
Sift the confectioners' sugar and cornstarch together into a shallow dish.
Roll the pieces of candy in the mixture.
Store the squares in boxes with more confectioners' sugar and cornstarch between each layer.

In *The Lion, the Witch and the Wardrobe*, Turkish Delight turns Edmund into a different person: it enslaves him. He loses all his senses and even betrays his brother and sisters. The Bible warns about things that enslave people: alcohol can do that, and the love for money. In today's world, drugs are like enchanted Turkish Delight—at first they make people feel good, but then they make them do foolish, hurtful things they would not ordinarily do. Even watching too much television can turn into a kind of "Turkish Delight" that can make you forget about being the sort of person God wants you to be.

Here is a prayer about avoiding things that are bad for you:

> *God, thank you that you love me and want me to be happy and healthy. I know you can help me, throughout life, to stay away from things that would make me foolish and unhappy. Thank you for protecting me.*

Aslan Is on the Move

In the land of Narnia it is always winter: snow and ice and cold, but never Christmas. If you live where winters are snowy, you might enjoy making snowmen, throwing snowballs, and sledding—but you would get sick of the season if it went on and on. Fortunately, this gloomy season does not last forever in Narnia. In *The Lion, the Witch and the Wardrobe*, the ice begins to thaw, and Father Christmas shows up.

What is the cause of this change? The talking beavers explain to the children, "Aslan is on

Following Aslan

the move." When the children hear this, they have mixed reactions. Peter feels brave and adventurous; Susan and Lucy are excited and happy; but Edmund (whom the witch has enchanted) is horrified.

When Jesus came into the world, people had similar reactions. For a long time, foreign armies had conquered the Holy Land, and God's people had been waiting for someone to rescue them from their unhappiness. Like Aslan, Jesus arrived at Christmas time—in fact, Christmas is Jesus's arrival into our world. After centuries of unhappiness, Christmas came, and "Aslan" began to move.

When Jesus grew up, he announced, "The Kingdom of God is at hand." The Kingdom of God is at hand in our lives, as well—or to put it in Narnia terms, Aslan is on the move. You don't see the Kingdom with your eyes, just like the children didn't see Aslan at first, but it is coming all around you. The Kingdom is coming whenever people choose to follow God. Aslan is on the move when children share their games or when they choose to listen to each other, because Jesus lives within them.

Just like in Narnia, some people in our world won't be happy when they hear Aslan—or Jesus—is on the move. Like Edmund, they may feel afraid if they hear Jesus is coming. They feel this way because they don't understand: if they knew how truly good he is, they would welcome the King into their lives. They hear he is a lion; they do not know what a good lion he is. Aslan's way is to win people's

Aslan Is on the Move

hearts through kindness. Our job is to accept people and care about them just the way they are.

A prayer about Aslan being on the move:

> *God, I thank you that you do not leave our world in wintry gloom but send your son to spread sunshine and warmth in our hearts. We thank you that the King is coming, and Aslan is on the move. We welcome him into our lives so we can be part of the change he wants to make in the world.*

The Lion Who Gave Himself Away

In *The Lion, the Witch and the Wardrobe*, Aslan, the wonderful Lion King of Narnia, offers his life to the evil White Witch, allowing her to tie him up and kill him with her stone knife. The good creatures in Narnia are grief-stricken, while the hags and werewolves laugh and rejoice. It seems as though the world has been turned terribly upside down—evil appears to have won. All this happens because of Edmund, the little boy from our world who chose to follow the witch instead of Aslan, and who betrayed his sisters and

The Lion Who Gave Himself Away

brother to the witch. The most amazing thing is that Aslan *chooses* to give himself to the witch, allowing her to tie him and kill him: and he does all that to free Edmund from the witch, despite all Edmund did. When reading the book or watching the movie you might have been troubled by all this. Why should Aslan do so much for Edmund? After all, Edmund doesn't seem very likeable.

Before you get too mad at Edmund, you might want to think again. Have you ever treated your brother or sister badly? I know, they do their share of annoying things—but perhaps your actions have not been entirely nice either. If we're really honest with ourselves, we've all done things that were selfish; we weren't thinking of anyone's happiness but our own. In a way, we've all been traitors to the people we care about, like Edmund was.

But like Edmund, we have a great King who loves us. In the same way that Aslan did, he willingly went to his death in order to buy us back from evil and make us his own dear children. "God demonstrates his own love for us in this: While we were still sinners, Christ died for us" (Romans 5:8). Aslan—or Jesus—loves us so much that he gave his life away.

The night before he goes to the witch, Aslan tells the girls, "I am sad and lonely." He asks them to put their hands on his mane and walk with him. If you read the Gospels in the Bible (Matthew, Mark, Luke, and John in the New Testament), you'll see that something similar happens there: the night before he dies on the cross, Jesus cries as he talks to God

Following Aslan

alone in a garden. He's lonely and sad, and he asks his friends to hang out with him and keep him company—but they fall asleep and leave him all alone on this terrible night.

Jesus was God's Son, but he also had human feelings. Thinking of what he would go through, he felt all the sad and scary emotions you or I would feel if we were facing something terrible—but he went ahead with what he chose to do because he loved us.

Thinking like this can make you feel sad, but it's also wonderful good news: the King loves you very much, and he will give himself away to make sure you're safe and happy.

A prayer about the King who gave his life away to show his love for you:

> *God, I know I have done some bad things, and when I think about those things I feel embarrassed and ashamed. But then I remember Jesus, and how much he loves me. I know you have forgiven me because of him. Thank you for sending your Son to pay the price for traitors like Edmund, and like me.*

The Stone Table

Chapter 14 of *The Lion, the Witch and the Wardrobe* tells about the most awful thing that happened in the land of Narnia: the death of Aslan, on an ancient stone table, at the hands of the witch. Mr. Lewis says, "The children did not see . . . the killing. They couldn't bear to look and had covered their eyes." I am sure if you were there, you would have covered your eyes also, as no one in their right mind would want to see something like this.

Following Aslan

Aslan's death seems even more awful because of what the witch says just before she plunges her knife into the Lion's heart. She claims she has won Narnia from the Lion. He gave his life to save the traitor Edmund, but who will protect Edmund after Aslan is gone? So the witch says, "You have given me Narnia forever." It is a truly awful moment. (If you have seen the movie or read the book, you know that the witch could not possibly have been more wrong. In fact, Aslan's death is the beginning of the end for the witch, but she doesn't know that yet.)

As he wrote about what happened on the stone table, Mr. Lewis was thinking about another death, one that happened a long time ago in our own world—the death of Jesus Christ. You have probably seen pictures of Jesus on the cross or perhaps statues that show Jesus hanging from a cross. Maybe you have even seen movies about how Jesus died. Like Aslan's death in Narnia, Jesus's death on the cross was an example of the most awful things that happen in our world. Unfortunately, we live in a world where people can be so cruel that they kill each other. They even killed Jesus.

When you see something so upsetting, you might ask yourself, why did it happen? Like Aslan, Jesus died to free someone; in fact, he died to set all people on earth free, so they could be close to God the way God had always wanted. Like the White Witch, the forces of evil in our world (what some people call the devil and his demons) thought they had

The Stone Table

won when Jesus died—but like the witch, they were totally wrong.

The Bible says that when he died, Jesus defeated the devil and his workers, "triumphing over them on the cross" (Colossians 3:15). When you think about Jesus dying on the cross, you will probably feel sad. Remember, though, that the death of Jesus (or the death of Aslan) is not the end of the story; the evil one may seem to be winning, but in fact, the forces of evil have just made a terrible mistake. God has just played his best trick; now he can begin to put the whole world right again because of what Jesus did on the cross.

A prayer about the stone table (and the cross):

> *God, thank you that your Son gave himself for me so that evil could be defeated. I will forever remember to be grateful.*

Deeper Magic

Bad times rarely last for long. Although we are sad about Aslan's death, what happens next in *The Lion, the Witch and the Wardrobe* is as joyous as can be. Susan and Lucy head back to the stone table, where they cry until no more tears are left. Then they see mice chewing away the cords that bind Aslan's body. Lucy remarks, "Poor little things—they don't realize he's dead. They think it will do some good untying him." They turn their faces away from the stone table to gaze at the sun rising over the royal palace, and at that moment, just as the sun comes up, they are surprised by a deafening noise behind them. The girls turn

Deeper Magic

around—and Aslan has returned to life! The risen King tells the girls how it happened: there is deeper magic than that of the Witch, magic set in place before time began. The deeper magic says that "when a willing victim who had committed no treachery was killed in a traitor's stead, the Table would crack and death itself would start working backwards." Aslan, filled with the energy of his new life, roars so loudly that all Narnia hears him. Then Lucy and Susan leap on his back for the most exciting ride of their life.

In the Gospels (the stories in the Bible about Jesus's life), Jesus's followers are heartbroken after he dies on the cross. They cry until they have no more tears. Meanwhile, the men who followed Jesus are hiding from everyone because they are afraid that the same people who killed Jesus will come after them. The women, however, go to Jesus's tomb, the way Susan and Lucy went back to see Aslan. There at the tomb, the women have the happiest experience they could imagine: an angel tells them, "Jesus is not dead, he is alive again—go tell his other followers!" Mary Magdalene, one of Jesus's followers, loves him even more deeply than the others, so she stays by the tomb after the others run back. Then something even more wonderful happens—Jesus appears and speaks her name: "Mary!" She wants to hug him and not let go, but Jesus tells her to go and tell the others that he is alive again. After that, Jesus appears to all his followers, both men and women, and he promises them, "I will always be with you as long as this world exists."

Following Aslan

The wonderful thing about Jesus is that he is not just some character out of history. You can read about Abraham Lincoln, or King Tut, or any other great historical figure, but you cannot talk to them, and they cannot hear you. They lived long ago, and you can see the tombs where they were buried. You could also see the tomb where Jesus was buried (if your parents were to take a very long trip to the Holy Land), but Jesus's tomb is very different from the others; it is empty. He is not there, because like Aslan, he rose back to joyous, powerful life! Jesus not only died for you, but he lives for you so that he can be your friend forever.

A prayer about the risen King:

Thank you, God, for raising your Son Jesus to life. Thank you that in our world, as well as Narnia, there is deeper magic from before the dawn of time. Thank you that Jesus now lives forever, to guide us, help us, protect us, and be our very best friend.

Dry Bones Live

If you recall in the beginning of *The Lion, the Witch and the Wardrobe*, when Mr. Tumnus the faun first meets Lucy, he is afraid of what the White Witch might do to him if she finds out he is hiding a human. Mr. Tumnus fears the witch might even turn him into a stone statue with a wave of her wand. In fact, that is exactly what happens, not only to Mr. Tumnus but also to many other good creatures. The witch's castle is filled with the trophies of her evil conquests: all kinds of beautiful animals and magical beings who have been transformed into cold, lifeless stone.

However, the deeper magic says that when a perfect being gives his life for a traitor, then "death itself would start working backwards." After Aslan roars, he begins to win Narnia back from the witch. One of the first things he does is leap into the witch's castle, and one by one, he breathes on the stone statues. The moment the Lion's breath touches them, the stone beings come back to life. The happiest moment for Lucy is when she finds her friend Mr. Tumnus, now a stone statue, and Aslan breathes him back to life. "A moment later Lucy and the little Faun were holding one another by both hands and dancing round and round for joy."

Have you ever known someone who died? Perhaps your grandfather or grandmother or someone else you care about got sick or had an accident and died. It can be very frightening and sad when that happens. If you go to a funeral, you might see the person you loved lying in a casket, and people come up to look and cry a little and say good-bye. Many of us have scared, unpleasant feelings when we go to a funeral, because when people die, they still look like themselves but they are cold, unmoving, like the stone statues in Narnia.

There is good news, however, in our world as well as in Narnia. Here, also, there is magic deeper than death. The only difference is that in our world, Aslan has not finished his work, so the stone statues still sleep—but they will not sleep forever!

In the Old Testament book of Ezekiel, the writer sees a valley filled with dry bones. God says to the bones, "I will make breath enter you, and you will

Dry Bones Live

come to life . . . I will put breath in you, and you will come to life. Then you will know that I am the Lord."

It is, as I said, scary and unpleasant when someone dies. We feel very sad, because we won't see the person we love for a long time. Yet death is not forever. The risen King will breathe on them, and they will return to life again. Like Lucy with Mr. Tumnus, you can look forward to a joyful reunion when Christ comes back and raises the dead to life again.

A prayer about the stone statues coming back to life:

> *God, you know how sad and scared I feel when I think about someone I love dying. Thank you that death is not the end of the story. Thank you that just as you raised Jesus back to life, so he will free all those who are captives of death. Thank you for that wonderful day when all those who sleep like cold statues now will return to joyful, warm life. Jesus, come soon, and blow the breath of life on those who now sleep in death. I look forward to that wonderful day.*

Aslan Is Bigger

Everyone learns from someone else; you learn from your parents and teachers, and perhaps you gain wisdom from talking to older adults like your grandparents or your aunt or uncle. Mr. Lewis, who wrote all the Narnia stories, also learned from an older wise man, a Scottish pastor and writer named George MacDonald. They never actually met, because George MacDonald lived before Mr. Lewis did, but Mr. Lewis read books by Mr. MacDonald, and he thought of the Scotsman as his teacher.

Aslan Is Bigger

George MacDonald said we should try to imagine the best things we can about God: think about all the ways that God is wise, lovely, beautiful, and good. Then, Mr. MacDonald said, we have to realize that God is "infinitely more" good than we can possibly imagine he is. The older we get, the more we can imagine—and yet God will always be still better and bigger than we can comprehend.

As you grow up, you will learn about many things. You will understand science and how the world works; you will learn about different kinds of people and their lives; you will learn to enjoy beautiful pictures and many different kinds of music. Most important of all, you can learn more and more about God and Jesus.

The more you learn about all these things, the bigger God and Jesus will become to you. As you learn more about the world God made, you will appreciate more the skill and goodness he put into making all this. The more you learn about other people and their ways, you will understand more about the love and the creativity of the God who made them all. The more you appreciate art and music, the more you will enjoy God who inspires all beauty.

Something similar happens in the second Narnia book, *Prince Caspian*, which tells the story of how the children return to Narnia. Although they have been in England for a short time, a long time has passed in Narnia. While the children were gone, people called the Telmarines have conquered Narnia,

Following Aslan

and they have driven the good animals and magical beings into hiding. The children team up with young Prince Caspian and help free Aslan's people from their enemies.

Several times, Lucy thinks that she sees a glimpse of Aslan, but the others do not believe her. Finally, Lucy meets Aslan in the woods. When she reaches the huge lion, she hugs him, buries her head in his enormous mane, and says, "Aslan, you're bigger." He tells her, "That is because you are older, little one." She asks if he has not actually grown larger, and Aslan assures her, "I am not. But every year you grow, you will find me bigger."

The same is true for you: the older you get, the bigger God appears—but you will never be smart enough (at least in this life) to understand all of his goodness. He is better than you can possibly imagine!

A prayer about a bigger view of Aslan:

> *God, you are almighty, you are all-knowing, and you are all-loving. Thank you for making me so that I can know and love you, at least in a small way. As I grow older and wiser, help me to love you more and more. May I always remember that you are even better than the best I can imagine you to be.*

Following Alone

In *Prince Caspian*, Lucy sees Aslan before her brothers and sister and Prince Caspian do. She wants to follow the Lion, but the others talk her out of doing so. When Lucy finally meets Aslan and speaks with him, the Lion gently reminds her that "much time has been lost" because she did not come to him at first. Lucy realizes an important truth: whether or not anyone else joins her, she must follow Aslan. She returns to the other children, telling them to come with

Following Alone

her and meet the Lion—and she adds that she will follow Aslan alone if they will not come with her.

An old song goes:

I have decided to follow Jesus,
No turning back, no turning back.
Though none go with me, I still will follow,
No turning back, no turning back.

This is the lesson Lucy learned: even if no one else follows Jesus, we must continue to follow him faithfully.

In the Gospels, Jesus makes clear that no matter what other people do, we must do what makes Jesus happy. That is not always easy. Especially as you get older, you may sometimes feel pressure to do what your friends are doing, even if they are doing bad things. Some kids begin smoking, shoplifting, or being rude to others simply because they want to "fit in" with people they think are their friends. (Of course, a *real* friend doesn't ask you to do something harmful.)

Whenever you have to make a choice in life, ask yourself, "If I do this, will I be following Jesus?" In other words, does Jesus want me to make this choice? If you are doing something helpful to other people, especially if you are being kind to people who are poor and hurting, then you can be sure you are following Jesus. If you are playing mean tricks on other people, calling them names and making them sad,

Following Alone

then you are not following Jesus. Jesus always acted in love—and he wants us to do the same.

Unfortunately, it's often easier to be mean when we are in a group. Have you ever heard this kind of remark: "Don't let Jessica sit here, we don't like her"? Or, "We don't want José on our team, he can't throw very good"? When you hear those kinds of things, you may have to follow Jesus alone. Say to your friends, "No! You're being mean to Jessica. I want to sit with her," or, "You're making José feel bad, and that's not right. We do want him on our team." It is not easy to follow Jesus alone. After all, you can see your friends, but Jesus is invisible. Nonetheless, he is there, and he is your real best friend, the one who will always be with you and always love you no matter what. And just like Lucy with Aslan, you'll find that the more closely you follow Jesus, the easier it will be to tell he is with you.

A prayer about following Jesus alone:

> *God, I know that Jesus is my real best friend, and doing what he wants matters more than what anyone else thinks. If my friends ask me to do wrong things, I know you will help me say "No" and do what Jesus wants instead. Help me to always have the courage to follow Jesus alone, even when that is difficult.*

Other Powers

In *Prince Caspian*, the prince finds himself in a war between the men who rule Narnia with cruelty and the talking animals and magical creatures who are faithful to Aslan. Partway through the story, Prince Caspian and his forces question whether they can win the war; their enemies are many more than they, and they have been defeated in battle over and over. At that point, the dwarf Nikabrik makes a horrible suggestion. Since they are losing the war, he says, "Either Aslan is dead or he is not on our side." Then

Other Powers

he says, "We want power," and reminds those listening to him that the White Witch had power when she ruled over Narnia in ancient times. Nikabrik has brought a werewolf and a lesser witch with him, and they begin a spell to raise the White Witch, but a brief fight stops their evil plan. If you remember how the White Witch behaved in *The Lion, the Witch and the Wardrobe*, you will realize what an awful idea Nikabrik had. Few things could be worse than bringing back the White Witch, and Nikabrik was wrong about Aslan: the Lion was already preparing to rescue his people.

From ancient times until today, people have tried to call up powers other than God to help them with their struggles. Today, some people still try to cast spells or do other things to get supernatural power—things the Bible says not to do. People who call up powers other than God sometimes get more than they bargained for: sometimes they get frightened.

We never have to be afraid of God; he is entirely good and only desires the best for his children. Sometimes we don't get our prayers answered the way we want them to be, or he waits a long time to answer our prayers—this is why Nikabrik suggested that Aslan was "dead or not on our side"—but God is very much alive and he does care. He knows what is best for us. But sometimes we may have to wait for his answer. And sometimes his answer is no.

We also know that Jesus is much greater than any other power people might turn to for help. In the Bible, the first letter by Jesus's disciple John says,

Following Aslan

"The reason the Son of God appeared was to destroy the devil's work." If you are on Jesus's side, you need never be afraid of other powers. Jesus is much greater and better than they are, and he is always watching over you to protect you.

A prayer about other powers:

> *God, thank you for sending Jesus into the world so he could put things right and undo the harm other spiritual powers might try to do. Protect the people who turn to sorcery or other supernatural things, and help them to turn instead to you. Thank you that I need never be afraid, and I can always trust Jesus to care for me.*

Healing and Happiness

Toward the end of *Prince Caspian*, Susan and Lucy once again ride on Aslan's back. Evil men have been ruling Narnia, but Aslan is putting everything right again. Talking animals and magical creatures join with the Lion and the children on a gleeful romp through the world of men. They come to a school where children have to wear uncomfortable outfits and learn the most boring history imaginable; the school dissolves as a girl named Gwendolen dances off with Aslan and the others. They

Following Aslan

see a man beating a boy with a stick; the man turns into a tree and the boy joins in the dance. Then they come to a house where a little girl is crying because her aunt is very sick, near death. The sick aunt sees Aslan and says, "Oh Aslan! I knew it was true. I've been waiting for this all my life. Have you come to take me away?" Aslan replies, "Yes, dearest, but not the long journey yet." Then he heals the woman, and she rides on the Lion's back. When they meet with Prince Caspian, he is overjoyed because the woman Aslan cured is Caspian's old nurse, whom he loved as a child.

Chapter 14 of *Prince Caspian* is great fun as Aslan and his followers travel across Narnia healing people, setting people free from those who mistreat them, and bringing happiness. That must have been what it was like when Jesus began his work on our earth, long ago. Jesus announced, "The Spirit of the Lord is on me, because he anointed me to preach good news to the poor. He has sent me to proclaim freedom for the prisoners and recovery of sight for the blind, to release the oppressed, to proclaim the year of the Lord's favor" (Luke 4:18–19). Like Aslan on his joyful romp through Narnia, Jesus did just as he said he would—he traveled through the Holy Land, curing people of their diseases, giving sight to the blind, and bringing happiness to people who were sad.

Jesus is still touching people today, even though you might not see him doing so. When we pray, he answers us. If you need Jesus to help set your world right side up, or you know someone who is hurting

Healing and Happiness

and needs Jesus's help, you only need to pray and ask for Jesus's assistance. Are you feeling unhappy? Ask Jesus to touch your heart and help you feel better. Do you have an illness that makes you feel miserable? Jesus will help you to get through your sickness, and he can help the doctors to make you better. Is someone being mean to you? Ask Jesus to help you love that person, while he helps him or her become a better person. You may have to look harder to see Jesus, but like Aslan on his romp through Narnia, Jesus is moving through our world today, bringing healing and happiness.

A prayer about healing and happiness:

> *God, you made us and you desire us to be happy and healthy. It makes me sad when I see people hurting—and sometimes the one hurting is me. Send Jesus wherever there is pain, and help hurting people to love him and open their lives to him. Come, Lord Jesus, and set right what is wrong in our world.*

At the End of Your Rope

At the end of *Prince Caspian*, Aslan is ready to make young Prince Caspian the next king over Narnia. Aslan asks Caspian, "Do you feel yourself sufficient to take up the kingship of Narnia?" Caspian replies, "I—I don't think I do, Sir, I'm only a kid." Aslan replies, "Good, if you had felt yourself sufficient, it would have been proof that you were not. Therefore . . . you shall be King of Narnia."

At the End of Your Rope

The first time you read *Prince Caspian* you might say to yourself, "Wait! Did I read that right?" It seems backward: Caspian doesn't feel ready to be king, therefore Aslan says that he is ready, but if Caspian had said, "Yes, Sir, I am ready to be king," then Aslan would have said, "No, you're not." What's going on here?

The Bible also says things that seem like contradictions at first glance. For instance, Jesus says, "Blessed are the poor in spirit, for theirs is the Kingdom of heaven." A new version of the Bible, *The Message*, translates the same saying of Jesus, "You're blessed when you're at the end of your rope. With less of you there is more of God and his rule." The Apostle Paul in his letter to the Christians in the city of Corinth wrote something nearly the same: "Brothers and Sisters, think of what you were when you were called. Not many of you were wise by human standards. . . . But God chose the foolish things of the world to shame the wise; God chose the weak things of the world to shame the strong."

You see, when people are overly proud of themselves, they don't think of asking God to help them. They think, "I'm smart, I'm strong—so why should I ask God to help me?" On the other hand, when people feel small or not very important, they're more likely to ask God for help. They get out of God's way and let him act through them. In the end, they often do better than people who try to live their lives without God's help.

Following Aslan

This is good news whenever you feel weak or unimportant. Do you feel like school is difficult, and you will need God to help you learn in your classes? That's okay, because if you look to God for help, he will help you—and you'll learn even more than you would otherwise. Are you feeling shy around people, afraid to meet new kids and make friends? Ask God to help, and he will show you how to meet kids who will be real friends. Whatever challenges you face, whether it is your family or sports or school or your friends, it is perfectly okay when you feel a little frightened, as though something is more than you can handle. Then you ask God to handle it for you. You'll be surprised. Things will turn out better than if you tried to do everything all by yourself.

A prayer about strength in weakness:

> *God, you know how sometimes I feel frightened about things. It is hard to begin a new sport, or go to a new school, or move to a strange place. When I feel small and unimportant, help me to do what I have to. I know when I call on you, you will help me, and things will turn out better than they would otherwise. Thank you for giving me strength when I feel weak.*

Where Your Treasure Is, There Is Your Heart

The third Narnia book, *The Voyage of the Dawn Treader*, introduces a new child: Eustace Scrubb, who travels to Narnia with his cousins, Lucy and Edmund. In Narnia, they find themselves on board a sailing ship, the *Dawn Treader*, which is traveling deep into the Narnian ocean under Prince Caspian's command as he searches for seven lost lords and for Aslan's country.

Following Aslan

From the beginning of the book, Eustace is an unlikable character. (Notice how much "Eustace" sounds like "Useless"?) He whines, complains, and insults other people. He is a spoiled brat whose mistakes land others in trouble. The way he behaves tells us he is not yet following Aslan.

Then, in the middle of the book, tragedy befalls Eustace. On a strange island, he disobeys orders and goes off by himself. He watches as an old, sickly dragon dies, and then he goes into the dragon's cave, which is filled with the dragon's hoard of treasure. Of course, Eustace starts thinking greedy thoughts about what he could do with such a treasure, but he is tired and falls asleep in the cave.

When he wakes up, he makes a terrible discovery: Instead of hands, he has claws. Instead of blowing air, he breathes fire. He is covered with scales, and he is now huge and ugly. Mr. Lewis explains for the reader, "Sleeping on a dragon's hoard with greedy, dragonish thoughts in his heart, he had become a dragon himself."

The love of wealth doesn't turn people in our world into dragons, but it can make people become ugly on the inside. Jesus preached a famous sermon that people call "the Sermon on the Mount," and in that sermon he said, "Do not store up for yourselves treasures on earth. . . . For where your treasure is, there your heart will be also." In the Bible, the Apostle Paul also warned his young friend Timothy, "The love of money is the root of all kinds of evil."

Where Your Treasure Is, There Is Your Heart

Most children sometimes wish they could have a better bike, a new video game system, or a bigger computer. Likewise, adults often dream of a more expensive car, a bigger house, or an expensive vacation. These desires are not bad in themselves (after all, bikes and computers, houses and vacations are all good things that God wants us to enjoy), but thinking too much about wanting these things can make us ugly inside. When we think, "I won't be happy if I don't get such and such," our thinking has become bent out of shape. We are no longer following Jesus, who told his followers, "The happy life does not depend on the things you own."

How can you guard yourself against the love of money? For starters, learn to share your things. Also, remember it is more fun to make other people happy by giving them gifts than it is to get gifts yourself. Most of all, remember the things that really make life happy—the love of other people and the love of God.

A prayer about treasure and our hearts:

> *God, my heart is so easily captured by the things the world holds. Help me to enjoy your gifts without depending on them for my happiness. Remind me of the really important things, like you, my family, and my friends. Help me to be generous, to enjoy giving gifts and sharing my things. Show me how to keep my treasure in the place where you want my heart to be.*

New Life

After poor Eustace is turned into a dragon, for a moment he thinks it might be fun to have everyone be afraid of him. Have you ever felt so angry at your family or teachers that you thought, "It would be fun to be a monster"? When our life feels out of control and people aren't treating us the way we'd like, all of us feel angry and frustrated—and we may wish we had the power to hurt people the way we have been hurt. However, Eustace very quickly

New Life

learns it is not much fun to be a monster. He can't do any of the things he enjoys; he can't hang out with people, and he misses human company very much. As a dragon, Eustace tries to help the *Dawn Treader* crew the best he can, bringing a tree for the broken mast, hunting, and scouting. He could have done none of these things when he was a boy (even if he had wanted to), but he still wishes very much he could turn back into his old self.

Then he meets Aslan. The Lion asks the dragon to follow him, and together they climb up a high mountain. At the top of the peak is a garden and pool. Aslan takes his claw, cuts into Eustace's dragon skin, and peels it off like the skin of a banana. Then he throws Eustace into a pool—and Eustace is a boy again, with his own body and face. When Eustace comes out of the pool, Aslan dresses him in a new set of clothes and sends him back to meet the others.

If you recall, until now in this book, Eustace has not been very likable. He always whines and complains and treats others poorly. He thinks he is smarter than others and acts like a snob. But after Aslan rescues him from his dragon nature, Eustace is a whole new person. He is much kinder, braver, and humbler, and other people like him much better.

Like many other things in *The Chronicles of Narnia*, the story of Eustace changing his dragon skin represents a spiritual reality—what the Bible calls "new birth." In the Gospel of John, when a wise man named Nicodemus (you say that like Nick-oh-deem-us) comes to ask Jesus's advice, Jesus tells him, "You must be born again." Nicodemus says, "What? I can't climb back into my mother's stomach." Jesus then explains that he is talking about a spiritual birth, a new beginning. Likewise, the Bible says, "If anyone is in Christ she is a new creation."

If we ask Jesus to come into our lives, he will. That means we must let go of our selfishness and open our hearts to love. We won't see a physical change, like Eustace did when he lost his dragon skin, but there will be a change on the inside. Like Aslan peeling away Eustace's dragon nature, God will begin to take away the selfish and mean parts of our characters. Just as Aslan gave Eustace new clothes, God will begin to give us new natures, more like his own.

A prayer about new life:

> *God, I know I haven't lived the way I should or treated others as nicely as I ought. I ask Jesus to come into my heart and change me. Start making me a new person, one who loves others and loves you. Thank you that you can change me.*

Growing Into a New Person

Eustace doesn't change entirely or all at once. Mr. Lewis says, "It would be nice, and fairly nearly true, to say that 'from that time forth Eustace was a new boy'. . . . He had relapses. . . . But . . . the cure had begun." For the rest of the book, we see that Eustace is slowly changing. Sometimes, when things are going very badly, Eustace acts like his old self, complaining or being

Following Aslan

cross with other people on the *Dawn Treader*. However, he also does some very brave things—like attacking a sea serpent—and he treats the other children with much more respect than he did before.

In the same way, when a child makes a decision to follow Jesus, a change begins. She will not change overnight, but gradually, she'll begin to show a new and different attitude. When a child begins trying to live like Jesus, the things he thinks are important will change. He wants to learn to know God better, so he will think about God and pray more. He will be kinder to others; she will try not to be so selfish. They may want to go to church or Sunday school, places where they can learn from other followers of Jesus. They try to help people and make things better in the world.

The Bible says that people who become new creatures in Christ Jesus will begin to show the fruits of the Spirit: "love, joy, peace, patience, gentleness, goodness, faith, humbleness, self-control" (Galatians 5:22,23). If you open your heart to Jesus, he will change you. It won't happen all at once, but slowly, you'll become less and less selfish, more and more generous; less mean, more gentle; less angry and more happy.

A prayer about growing into a new person:

> *God, thank you that I can become a better person than I am now. Forgive me for times when*

Growing Into a New Person

I'm unkind or selfish, and forgive me for times when I don't listen to you or serve you like I should. Change me, day by day, into the new person you want me to be. Thank you for making me gradually more like your Son, Jesus.

Never Give Up

Many readers of *The Voyage of the Dawn Treader* agree their favorite character is Reepicheep, the valiant mouse. We expect mice to be timid creatures, tiny little things that point their noses at us from underneath the furniture, then run and hide in the attic. However, Narnia is a magical realm, and things in Aslan's country are often the opposite of what we expect in our own. Reepicheep dresses fashionably, always wearing his sword, speaks like a knight in armor, and is always the bravest member of the

Never Give Up

Dawn Treader crew. When threatened by a dragon, a sea serpent, or human enemies, Reepicheep is the first to attack. He never runs from danger, and he politely but firmly reminds others to be brave when they are afraid.

Reepicheep is not only brave, but he has also made up his mind to seek Aslan. Prince Caspian is sailing into the far ocean in search of seven missing nobles from his father's court, but Reepicheep has a deeper reason for the journey. The brave mouse is determined to reach Aslan's country and stay there. That's probably why he is so brave, for the Bible tells us that "perfect love casts out fear." In other words, if you're thinking about loving God or others, you won't have as much room in your thoughts for feeling scared.

In one scene, the crew suggests that perhaps the *Dawn Treader* should turn around and head back to their homeland. Reepicheep will not go along with them: it is unthinkable that he stop short of his goal. The valiant rodent explains, "My own plans are made. While I can, I sail east in the *Dawn Treader*. When she fails me, I paddle east in my coracle. When she sinks, I shall swim east with my four paws. And when I can swim no longer, if I have not reached Aslan's country . . . I shall sink with my nose to the sunrise."

Reepicheep will never quit doing his best, and he will never stop short of his goal. He will give every ounce of energy to reach Aslan's country, and he will die trying if need be. We cannot help but admire this utterly determined mouse.

The Bible has a word for never giving up until you reach your goal: *perseverance*. The New Testament book of James says, "We count as blessed those who have persevered!" No matter what your goals are, you will need perseverance to accomplish them. To learn well in school, you will need perseverance. When people are mean to you, and you have to get along with them somehow, you will need perseverance. Most important, in following God you will need perseverance. Like Reepicheep the noble mouse, never quit doing your very best, and by perseverance you will reach your goals.

A prayer for perseverance:

> *God, you know life can be hard. I don't always want to do homework for school, or practice for sports, or be nice to my brother or sister. But I know you can help me to keep trying my hardest. Give me the gift of perseverance, so I can achieve the dreams you have for my life.*

The Way to Aslan's Country

At the end of *The Voyage of the Dawn Treader,* Prince Caspian, his crew, and the children from our world do reach Aslan's country and meet the great Lion himself. Aslan tells the children,

Following Aslan

"For you, the door into Aslan's country is from your own world." Edmund is surprised and says, "What! Is there a way into Aslan's country from our world too?" Aslan replies, "There is a way into my country from all worlds." Lucy asks, "Will you tell us how to get into your country from our world?" and Aslan says, "I shall be telling you all the time."

In writing *The Chronicles of Narnia*, Mr. Lewis hoped that his stories would help children meet the Great King, the one who died for the Sons of Adam and Daughters of Eve, the one who rose to life again. On the very last page of *Dawn Treader*, Aslan says, "This was the very reason you were brought to Narnia, that by knowing me here for a little, you may know me better there."

There are indeed many ways into Aslan's country from our world, and Aslan is "telling us all the time" how we can meet him. In a book called Acts, the Bible tells of a day when the Apostle Paul, one of Jesus's special messengers, spoke to the people of ancient Greece and said, "From one man he [God] made every nation . . . , that they should inhabit the whole earth; and he determined the times set for them and the exact places where they should live. God did this so that [people] would seek him and perhaps reach out for him and find him, though he is not far from each one of us. 'For in him we live and move and have our being.'"

Grown-ups sometimes say, "If Jesus is real, then why doesn't he speak to everyone?" In fact, Jesus *is*

The Way to Aslan's Country

speaking, calling children, women, and men to come and enjoy his love. He does not just speak in churches or Sunday school (if that were the case, many people would never hear him, since not everyone goes to church or Sunday school). The Bible says God speaks to people in nature; when you see a beautiful forest, majestic mountain, or roaring ocean wave, you can feel close to God: the beauty of nature shows us the beauty of God. God also speaks to people through special books and movies like *The Chronicles of Narnia* or *The Lord of the Rings* by J. R. R. Tolkien. (You might have to wait until you are a little older to read Tolkien's books, but you will enjoy them if you like the Narnia books.) Popular bands also sing about God and how his love has helped them to be better people; all kinds of music can help people feel closer to God. And of course, God speaks through the books of the Bible; they are his special words. Even though not everyone hears, in many different ways Aslan is calling people to himself, all the time. Sometimes, we just have to take time to listen.

A prayer about the way to Aslan's country:

> *God, open my ears to hear and my eyes to see where Jesus is calling to me. Help me to help others hear him as well.*

Aslan's Call

Book four of *The Chronicles of Narnia* is *The Silver Chair*. At the start of the book, bullies are chasing two British schoolchildren, Eustace (called Scrubb in this book) and a new girl in the series, Jill Pole (also known simply as Pole), when Eustace calls out to Aslan for help—and the two children find themselves transported into Narnia. As the story goes on, they will help to release the

Aslan's Call

prince of Narnia from a magical spell cast by another evil witch. First, however, Jill Pole has to learn about Narnia; of course, she is surprised being suddenly picked up from her normal life at school in England and dropped into a whole new magical world.

When she first arrives in Narnia, Jill meets Aslan. She explains to him that Eustace called for Aslan, and that is how they arrived here. Aslan then tells her, "You would not have called to me unless I had been calling to you." Perhaps that part of the story puzzled you. Who is calling whom, here? What is Aslan talking about?

Mr. Lewis is again expressing an idea from the Bible, where it talks a lot about how God is always "calling" human beings to himself. Jesus told his followers, "You did not choose me but I chose you."

You may not have thought about it this way before. If you have made a decision to follow Jesus, you probably felt as though this was a choice *you* made. However, you could not have made that choice if *something*—either something outside of you like your mom or your Sunday school teacher or a book you were reading, or something inside of you like a feeling or a strong thought—did not pull you toward Jesus. It is like Aslan from the land of Narnia, calling Pole and Scrubb to come from their world to his. As he says to the children: "You would not have called to me unless I had been calling to you."

The one thing certain is this: God loved you before you even thought about loving him back. He was thinking about you before it occurred to you to think of him.

A prayer about Aslan's call:

Thank you, God, for loving me even before I was born. It is awesome to think you care about me so much. Thank you for calling me, so I could respond to you and become your friend.

Aslan's Signs

In *The Silver Chair*, when Jill Pole meets Aslan, she finds he has a mission for her. In *The Chronicles of Narnia*, whenever Aslan calls children from our world to his, there is important work for them to do, and this is certainly the case in *The Silver Chair*. Pole and Scrubb have to save Narnia from an underground invasion threatened by the Emerald Witch.

To complete Aslan's mission and rescue Narnia from evil, the children must follow a set of "signs" Aslan gives them. He tells Jill, "remember, remem-

Following Aslan

ber, remember the Signs. Say them to yourself when you wake in the morning and when you lie down at night. . . . And whatever strange things may happen to you, let nothing turn your mind from following the signs." Later on in the book, their new friend Puddleglum tells the children, "Aslan's instructions always work: there are no exceptions." Of course, Aslan's instructions always work, as long as people remember to follow them! In *The Silver Chair*, there are times when the children follow the signs and things go well . . . and there are times they forget to follow the signs and things go badly.

By now you've realized that many things in Mr. Lewis's stories have parallels (something that's sort of the same) in our world. So what would Aslan's signs be in our own world? The first thing that comes to my mind are the Ten Commandments, which God gave to Moses and which Christians and Jews still try to follow today. Here is a simple form of the Ten Commandments:

1. Put God first.
2. Worship only God.
3. Use God's name with respect.
4. Remember God's Sabbath (a day of rest when we take time to think about God).
5. Respect your parents.
6. Don't hurt others.
7. Be faithful in marriage.
8. Don't steal.
9. Don't lie.
10. Don't be envious of others.

Aslan's Signs

When Jesus came into our world, he taught his followers a simple way to know if they were following God's signs: "Treat others the way you want them to treat you." This simple rule (sometimes called the Golden Rule) sums up the Ten Commandments in a single sentence. In everything you do, if you stop to repeat Jesus's "sign," you will find his path is much easier to follow—and you too (like Scrubb and Pole) can accomplish Aslan's mission in our world.

A prayer about Aslan's signs:

> *God, you gave us your rules to keep us safe and happy. Help me to love and follow your signs throughout life, and to encourage others to do so as well. Thank you for allowing me to help put your hurting world right again, as I follow your commandments.*

Following Aslan

By the middle of chapter 5, the children in *The Silver Chair* are thinking their Narnia adventure is not as much fun as they thought it would be. They are on a mission to rescue Prince Rilian from the Emerald Witch, but even getting to the witch's kingdom is a difficult task. It is a long trip, and they are cold and hungry. They make an unlikely friend, Puddleglum the marshwiggle, but he is a glum character, always thinking of unhappy things that might happen to them all.

Following Aslan

As they enter the land of the giants, Puddleglum starts listing all the unfortunate things that are likely to happen to them, but Eustace replies, "I don't think Aslan would ever have sent us if there was so little chance as all that." Although many awful things happen to the party, the children keep from giving up because they know Aslan has called them. There is a purpose for their time in Narnia.

In the same way, Jesus has a purpose for you in our world. In the Bible, the book of Ephesians tells us, "We are God's workmanship, created in Christ Jesus to do good works, which God prepared in advance for us to do." God has a plan for your life! What is that plan? You will have to find that out for yourself. It could be a thousand different things. Maybe he wants you to become a scientist who will discover the cure for a terrible disease, enabling many people to live longer, happier lives. Maybe he wants you to become a teacher, helping children to achieve an education and do better in the world as a result. Maybe he wants you to become a musician, making people happier when they listen to your CDs or your shows, or he wants you to become an artist whose paintings will show people what beauty is and lead them to God that way. Or maybe he wants you to be a just leader who will help others make wise decisions.

I don't mean to suggest that following God's purpose will always make someone famous or rich. In fact, God seems to do more good in the world through

Following Aslan

ordinary people who never become well known or make a lot of money; those may be the sorts of people he especially enjoys. (After all, plenty of rich and famous folks do very little good for other people.) But whether you are known or unknown, whether your house and your bank account are big or small, Jesus wants you to love him, follow his signs, and treat other people the way you want to be treated. Whatever you believe God calls you to do, do it gladly with all your heart, knowing that God will help you make the world a better place.

A prayer about Aslan's call:

> *Thank you, God, for making me for a purpose: thank you that you created me to do "good works." Help me to discover things I am good at doing, that please you, and that help other people. And when I have found your purpose for my life, help me to follow it gladly, knowing that you will never lead me the wrong way.*

The Blood of Aslan

At the end of *The Silver Chair*, King Caspian, a favorite character with many readers of *Prince Caspian* and *The Voyage of the Dawn Treader*, has died of old age. The children and Aslan find his body lying on the golden gravel of a stream on Aslan's mountain. The Lion and the children all cry together.

Then Aslan tells Eustace to break off a gigantic thorn, a foot long and sharp as a sword, and thrust the thorn into his paw. "Eustace set his teeth and drove the thorn into the lion's pad. And there

Following Aslan

came out a great drop of blood, redder than all redness that you have ever seen or imagined." Aslan's blood pours into the stream containing Caspian's dead body—and suddenly, Caspian leaps up from the water, alive again!

The children are astonished, and they ask Aslan: "Hasn't Caspian died?" Aslan replies, "Yes, he has died. Most people have, you know. Even I have." However, the blood of Aslan, the king who died and rose again, has power to bring the dead back to life.

I don't know about you, but I am squeamish when it comes to blood. The last time I gave blood, I looked at the little plastic tube coming out of my arm and fainted. It was very embarrassing; I woke up and didn't even know what had happened. Sometimes I visit people in the hospital, and I have to leave their room because I see blood and feel sick. You might feel the same way. God made our bodies so that the blood stays inside of us, and when we see it bleeding out, we know something is wrong. After all, blood is what helps keep every part of our bodies alive and healthy.

So you might say, blood is a very powerful thing. When you think about it like that, it makes sense that Aslan's blood (or Jesus's) would have great power to bring life and healing. The Bible tells us Jesus was happy because he was able "to reconcile to himself all things, whether things on earth or things in heaven, by making peace through his blood, shed on the cross" (Colossians 1:20). When Jesus died, it was a terrible day for his followers. They cried as

The Blood of Aslan

they watched someone they loved get hurt so badly. However, Jesus chose to go to the cross and shed his blood there so he could win back all people to God and show his love for the world. On the last day, when all the dead rise to life and stand before God, they will be raised from death through the power of Jesus's blood.

A prayer about the blood of Aslan:

> *God, thank you that you loved me so much that you sent your Son to give his blood for me. It makes me sad to think that Jesus did this. Yet I am deeply grateful, knowing that I have peace with you and I will be raised to life by the blood of Jesus.*

Aslan Watches Over Us

The fifth of *The Chronicles of Narnia* is *The Horse and His Boy*, which tells the story of Shasta, a poor boy in the land of Calormen, who is badly treated by a man who claims to be his father (but isn't really). Shasta meets a talking horse who convinces him to run away and try to reach Narnia. At this time, Lucy, Edmund, Susan, and Peter are reigning as kings and queens in Narnia.

The Horse and His Boy is unusual because Aslan doesn't come into the story until almost the end of the book—or actually, we don't realize Aslan

Aslan Watches Over Us

is in the story until we get toward the end. When Shasta finally meets Aslan, the Great Lion explains how he has been watching over the boy since he was born. Aslan pushed the boat that held Shasta when he was a baby, so it would go safely to shore. Aslan took the form of a cat when Shasta was lonely and afraid. Aslan was a lion that chased Shasta's horse in order to hurry him forward at time when Narnia was threatened. In many ways that the boy never realized, Aslan has been protecting and helping him throughout life.

The beginning of John's Gospel speaks of Jesus saying, "He was with God in the beginning. Through him all things were made. . . . In him was life, and that life was the light of all people." This means that Jesus's light and life touches everyone, whether they know it or not. In Psalm 139, King David prays:

> *O Lord, you have searched me and you know me.*
> *You know when I sit and when I rise; you perceive my thoughts from afar.*
> *You discern my going out and my lying down:*
> *You are familiar with all my ways.*

You may not always be thinking about Jesus, but he is always thinking about you. There may have been times in your life when you did not even know you were in danger, and he secretly protected you.

Following Aslan

Whether you are happy or sad, angry or kind, lonely or in a crowd, Jesus is there with you.

A prayer about Aslan watching over you:

> *Thank you, God, for the constant presence of your Son Jesus in my life. He has always been with me, whether I knew it or not, guiding and protecting me. Help me to think of him more often, even as he constantly thinks of me.*

A True King

At the end of *The Horse and His Boy*, Shasta learns his true identity. Early in the story, he met a boy his age named Prince Corin, who looked exactly like him. At the end of the story, Shasta learns he is really Prince Cor, Corin's identical twin, who was separated from him at birth—and it turns out, Cor is the heir to the throne of an entire kingdom called Archenland.

Following Aslan

His true father, King Lune, explains what it means to rule a kingdom: "For this is what it means to be a king: to be first in every desperate attack and last in every desperate retreat, and when there's hunger in the land (as must be now and then in bad years) to wear finer clothes and laugh louder over a scantier meal than any man in your land." No wonder Shasta's brother Corin is delighted to discover he doesn't have to be king!

Many things in Aslan's kingdom seem upside down from our way of thinking. Why should the king put himself in the greatest danger during war? In today's army, the generals sit at computer stations miles away from danger (and prime ministers and presidents seldom go anywhere near the fighting). Why should the king get the smallest meal if people in his land are hungry? Presidents today live very richly compared to most people in the country. If someone told you, "You are going to live like a king," you would probably think, "Hooray, I am going to be rich!" But that isn't what it means to be king in Aslan's country.

In Mark's Gospel, there is a story about the time when two of Jesus's followers argue about who was greatest. Jesus calls all twelve of his followers together and sits them down to listen to him. He tells them, "Anyone who wants to be first must be the very last, and the servant of all." That is how Jesus himself lived. Although he was rich as God, he became a poor human being. Although he made the

A True King

world, he allowed evil people in the world to take him captive. Although he gives life to all people, he allowed people to take his life from him. Jesus was the Son of God, yet he put the happiness of other people before his own happiness.

All of us enjoy being the leader sometimes. It's fun to have other people listen to our ideas and put them into action. And it may be that you do have very good ideas. Just keep in mind Jesus's idea of leadership. Being a good leader is just the opposite of being bossy or selfish.

A prayer about the way a true king behaves:

> *God, you created everything through your Son Jesus, yet he came to earth and became poor so that others might be happy and free. Sometimes I like to boss people around and tell them what to do. Forgive me when I do that, because that is not the way a true leader behaves. Help me to be a true leader, who helps people instead of bossing them.*

The Beginning

The *Magician's Nephew*, book six in *The Chronicles of Narnia*, is one of the wildest and most fun of the Narnia books. Unlike the others, it takes place a long time ago, before automobiles or electricity. In it, Mr. Lewis introduces two new characters, Polly and Digory. Digory's uncle is an evil magician, who sends the two children to Narnia, where they meet the White Witch when she first came to Narnia at the dawn of time.

The highlight of *The Magician's Nephew* is the creation of Narnia. Aslan walks back and forth

The Beginning

singing, and as he sings, the land of Narnia "spread out from the Lion like a pool." From the Lion's mouth comes forth flowers, trees, and other plants. Then, little bubbles rise from the surface of the new earth, and as they burst, the animals come out.

There is nothing quite as wonderful as standing on a beach and looking out across the ocean, watching the waves form as if by magic, sweep across the face of the deep, and go "whoosh!" into foam at the shore. Likewise, it is a glorious thing to stand on top of a mountain, up close to the sky and clouds, and breathe in the cool, pure air and look across miles of land in every direction. Maybe you love the little simple things in nature, like catching grasshoppers or chasing rabbits as they play in the bushes.

God did an awesome job creating our world! Genesis chapter 1 tells how God said, "Let there be," and like Aslan singing Narnia into existence, the world came forth. As he created each thing—land and ocean, sea creatures, and animals—God said, "It is good!" Then, when he made the first people, God was even more pleased and he called them "very good!" Adults can get into all kinds of arguments about exactly how and when this all happened, and that is rather sad, because however it happened and however long it took, the end result is a world that's beautiful and wonderful and amazing.

Have you ever gone to a zoo? As you see all the interesting creatures that live on our planet, give thanks to the Creator who displays such creativity and skill. Maybe you have a pet, a dog or a cat, a hamster or even a fish; as you care for your pet, you may be surprised to find that God shows himself to you in the way an animal makes you laugh or feel loved. Whether you are by the ocean, in a forest, high up on a mountain, or in the middle of a city looking up at the sky, take time to notice the might and splendor of the Maker who produced such wonderful things.

A prayer about Creation:

> *Creator, when I look at the starry skies, the rolling oceans, and majestic mountains, it takes my breath away. I'm glad for animals, for trees and grass, for everything you've made. Thank you for creating such an amazing world and for letting me live in it.*

Keeping Our Word

In chapter 13 of *The Magician's Nephew*, Digory faces a terrible choice. At the beginning of the story, Mr. Lewis told us that Digory's mother is very sick, even near death. Now, the boy hopes desperately that he can save his mother by finding some magical cure in Narnia.

Soon after Aslan created Narnia, the Lion sent Digory on a flying horse to bring back "the apple of life" from a garden atop a mountain. When he reaches the garden, the boy meets the witch, who tells him he should take the fruit and go back to England rather than return to Aslan. By doing so, the witch says, he can save his mother's life. If he went back to England instead of obeying Aslan, who would know? Which is more important, asks the witch, obeying Aslan or going directly to his ailing mother?

Although Digory wants very much to get help for his mother, he decides to take the fruit back to Aslan. He tells the witch, "I promised." After he brings the fruit back to Aslan, the Lion tells him that if he had broken his promise and done as the witch suggested, the fruit would indeed have healed his mother—yet something else would have happened, something so bad that Digory and his mother would both have regretted it horribly. However, after he brings the fruit to the Lion, Aslan allows him to take an apple to his mother, who recovers, and they live happily after that.

As Digory discovered, it can be difficult keeping one's promise. If you are going to get in trouble for something you did, you might be tempted to lie. Sometimes, people say they will do something just to make someone happy or get something for themselves, but they don't intend to do what they say.

The Bible says God will bless people "who keep their promise even when it hurts" (Psalm 15). If you are tempted to break a promise, think: "What if everyone decided to break their promises?" It would be a sad world, wouldn't it?

Keeping Our Word

There are only a few, a *very few* cases where you should allow yourself to break a promise. Maybe you saw someone do something very, very bad, and that person forced you to promise not to tell or else he or she would hurt you. That is not a real promise, because you made the promise out of fear, not out of your own desire. If someone is doing mean things to you or making you do things you are ashamed of, you need to tell your parents, your teacher, or some adult you trust. God understands if you break a so-called promise like that.

In all other cases, God wants us to do whatever we say. This is one way we can become more like him, because God always keeps his promises. Everything he promises in the Bible, he brings to pass. Anything God has said he will do for you, he will fulfill. We can trust him to keep his promises, and he will help us to keep our promises as well.

A prayer about keeping your word:

> *God, thank you that I can trust you. Help me, in turn, to be honest and dependable, someone who can be counted upon to do just what I say.*

Unable to Hear

One of the characters in *The Magician's Nephew* is Digory's magician uncle, Andrew, who messes around with sorcery; not knowing what he is doing, he releases the White Witch into Narnia—and into England as well. Uncle Andrew is stupid and conceited, and one of the saddest things about him is that he cannot hear Aslan's voice: even if the Lion is right next to him speaking, Uncle Andrew only hears wild beast sounds. Aslan would like to talk to Uncle Andrew so he could be a happier, kinder person, but the Lion

Unable to Hear

explains, "I cannot comfort him . . . he has made himself unable to hear my voice."

Have you ever had the experience of saying something to an adult, and they just don't hear you? Or maybe they say, "Yes, yes," but you know they are not thinking about what you said at all. They are thinking grown-up thoughts, so even though you are making sounds right next to them, they don't hear you.

In Matthew 13:15, Jesus says, "For this people's heart has become calloused; they hardly hear with their ears, and they have closed their eyes." There are many people, both children and adults, who don't listen for Jesus's voice. God is speaking to people all the time, calling them to love him, asking them to make good decisions. Unfortunately, some people are caught up in their own world, thinking busy thoughts, not hearing what God says to them.

God doesn't usually speak as a voice you can hear coming out of thin air, like he spoke to Moses in the Bible. He doesn't usually communicate like he did in the television show *Joan of Arcadia*, where different people told Joan they were God's voice. But we can hear God speak to us in the Bible, in the wise words of parents and other people who care about us, in the wind and birdsong, in a cat's purr and the sound of our friends' laughter. Sometimes he speaks very quietly in our feelings, and we hear him with the ears of our heart.

If you ask him to guide you, God will give you direction in life. If you want to learn how to hear

Following Aslan

God's voice, God will teach you to do that. You just have to pray . . . and listen.

A prayer about hearing Aslan's voice:

God, thank you for promising to give me direction when I need it. Help me to listen and help me to learn to hear your voice guiding me.

Hurting People

The final book in *The Chronicles of Narnia* is *The Last Battle*, a glorious conclusion to the series. In this story, a huge problem begins with a tiny incident (as sometimes happens in real life as well): a talking ape named Shift finds the skin from a lion that hunters killed. Shift takes advantage of a not-so-bright donkey named Puzzle, forcing Puzzle to dress in the skin and impersonate Aslan. Shift then makes a deal with the Calormen rulers. (If you have read many of these books, you know the Calormen are enemies of the Narnians.)

Following Aslan

At this time, Tirian is king of Narnia. (He is unaware that in fact he is the very last king of Narnia.) When Tirian receives the news that someone is cutting down talking trees, he rushes to investigate. He finds that terrible things are happening in Narnia; talking animals and people have become slaves who must follow the orders of the Calormen soldiers and the talking ape, Shift. Shift has enslaved people by means of the donkey dressed in the lion skin. Shift tells people that Aslan has returned, and they must do what Aslan orders them to do.

King Tirian soon realizes that all this is a nasty trick; the real Aslan would not ask people to mistreat one another. However, Shift and the Calormen soldiers take Tirian by force and tie him up. Realizing that these imposters are taking over Narnia, Tirian calls on the real Aslan to come and save his kingdom.

In our world, sometimes people use Jesus's name to do terrible things. People can become confused and hurt each other, thinking they are following Jesus. When something like that happens, how can people know what Jesus wants them to do?

When Jesus was alive on earth, a man once asked him, "What must I do to gain eternal life?" Jesus told him, "Love God and love your neighbor the way you love yourself." Then the man asked, "Who is my neighbor?" Jesus told a story about a Samaritan—a hated enemy of the Jews—who helped a wounded Jew. The story showed that your neighbor is any person in need, even a person you do not like. Jesus

Hurting People

made it perfectly clear that his followers must always seek to help other people: he would never ask us to hurt anyone or be unkind. So if someone uses Jesus's name to do harm, we know we should not listen.

A prayer about hurting people in Aslan's name:

> *God, I know your Son loves all children and adults, and he would never ask his followers to hurt other people. Help those who lie in your name and try to hurt others. Protect others from being confused and help us all to follow Jesus truly.*

Being Our Own King

In *The Last Battle*, Shift the ape manages to get all the groups that live in Narnia mad at each other. Giving orders through the false Aslan, Shift invites the Calormen army to take over Narnia. A battle follows, in which the talking animals and loyal Narnians fight against Shift and his forces.

The dwarfs have their own army, and King Tirian begs the dwarfs to join him in the battle against evil. However, the dwarfs have no interest in joining either side. They tell the king, "We're on our own now. No more Aslan, no more kings, no

Being Our Own King

more stories about other worlds. The Dwarfs are for Dwarfs." Throughout the book, they repeat that saying, "The Dwarfs are for Dwarfs." Toward the end of the story, something strange happens: because they will not follow Aslan, the dwarfs cannot see or hear him. Like Digory's Uncle Andrew in *The Magician's Nephew*, the dwarfs have made themselves deaf to Aslan's voice. Even when they have the chance to enter Aslan's land, the dwarfs refuse to do so: they have chosen to rule themselves rather than accept Aslan as their king.

At the beginning of the Bible, in the book of Genesis, when Adam and Eve choose to turn away from following God, they do so because the serpent tells them, "You will be like God." Sin happens when a person says, "I don't need God. I will be my own God and do what I think is right." Whenever we make ourselves the center of our world, we leave no room for God's love.

Grown-ups find all sorts of reasons for making themselves the center of the world, and some of these reasons sound pretty good. They might say, "I'm just looking out for number one," or, "It's healthy to take care of myself," or, "If I don't look out for myself, no one else will." There's just enough truth in these statements that people don't have to see that they're really finding an excuse to be selfish. They're like the dwarfs who are determined to take care of their own interests first—and just as the dwarfs became deaf to Aslan's voice, these people can't hear Jesus.

While they claim to find freedom, they are actually missing real happiness.

Individuals can put themselves at the center of the world, but so can groups of people. Whenever we draw a line between "us" and "them," we are in danger of falling into the dwarfs' mistake. The problems on our planet are mostly due to people who say, "We're for us and us only." There are all sorts of ways to say that: "We girls are for girls and girls only," for instance, and, "We boys are for boys only," or, "White kids are for white kids only," or, "We black kids are for black kids only." Whenever we say we only care about "us" and not "them," we've forgotten that not only does God love us all, but we're all connected to each other. If we refuse to let Jesus be our king, we not only hurt each other, we hurt ourselves.

Real happiness—what Jesus calls "the abundant life"—is following Jesus as king and allowing his love to enter our lives. Those who try to be their own king are bound to fail, because we all need God's help to deal with all the difficult things in this world. Jesus is a *good* king, so whatever he asks of us he asks for our own happiness. If everyone followed Jesus's instructions, our world would be a peaceful, happier place.

A prayer about being our own king:

> *God, I know you sent Jesus to our world so we could know what is right and live peacefully the way you desire. Show the people who want to be*

Being Our Own King

their own king to realize they are only hurting themselves. Help me to notice when I'm making myself the center of the world, and remind me to make room for you, so that your Son can be my king.

What the Stable Held

The final chapters of *The Last Battle* are full of wonderful ideas that will stay in your head for a long time. One of them is a stable that contains an entire world inside of it, a world that is actually bigger than Narnia. This raises a fascinating question: how can this tiny building contain something larger than the world it rests on? Lucy remarks that, "In our world too, a Stable once had something inside it that was bigger than our whole world."

We think of that stable every year around Christmastime. One of my favorite things is a nativity

What the Stable Held

set that I have had for almost forty years. When I was a little boy, my mother and father took me to a store and told me to pick out a little wooden stable and the figures to go in it. We started with a tiny baby Jesus lying on a bed of straw in a little plastic manger. Then we added his mother Mary, dressed in a blue shawl and staring with love at her baby boy, along with her husband Joseph, older, with a beard and staff, also gazing at the child. Then we bought the shepherds, some holding sheep, others resting on their shepherds' crooks. Finally, we bought three wise men; I loved these because they were African and Asian, adding variety to the little crowd of plastic people who inhabited the manger. Every year at Christmastime, I still unwrap the little nativity scene and set up the miniature stable that holds the baby Jesus.

Maybe you have a nativity set in your home at Christmastime. Perhaps your church has a life-sized stable and figures of the nativity that it puts out on the front lawn before Christmas. Some churches wait to put the baby Jesus in the manger until Christmas day, when they celebrate the Christ Child's birth. Maybe you have seen a living nativity: those are special because all the people and animals and even the baby are real.

Every Christmas, we see the stable and the baby Jesus; in fact, we've seen it so many times, that it no longer seems particularly amazing or remarkable. The Gospel of John, however, reminds us that Jesus created the world and everything in it—and then, "the Word [Jesus] became flesh and lived among us." That little baby in the stable is also God, who created the world! So the Christmas story is not just about the birth of a baby, like when you were born, or when your little sister was born. The story is much greater than an ordinary birth (as miraculous as every birth is). Like the stable in *The Last Battle*, the Christmas story raises the question: how could a tiny baby contain something larger than the world where he was born?

I can't give you the answer to that question. It's one of those questions that will challenge you and make you think for the rest of your life.

A prayer about what the stable held:

> *Thank you, God, for sending your Son to live on earth that first Christmas day. Thank you for the miracle of the stable that held something greater than the world! Fill my heart with wonder whenever I think about Jesus being born into our world.*

The End of the World

The *Last Battle* is not only the end of *The Chronicles of Narnia* series; it also tells about the end of Narnia itself, since all worlds (even our own) do end. However, the end of Narnia is also a new beginning—the beginning of the endless new world to come after Narnia. Before that new world can start, the world of Narnia has to come face to face with Aslan.

In chapter 14 of *The Last Battle*, a great crowd comes rushing out of the dying world of Narnia, "by thousands and by millions, came all kinds of creatures—Talking Beasts, Dwarfs, Satyrs, Fauns,

Following Aslan

Giants," and all the races of human beings in Narnia. Each of these creatures comes face to face with Aslan. As they do so, "one or the other of two things happened to them." Some looked at Aslan with fear or hatred: these individuals disappeared into Aslan's shadow. The children never saw these creatures again, and they did not know what actually became of them.

There were other creatures, however, who "looked in the face of Aslan and loved him." They went on into the new and wonderful world Aslan created, the world that replaced Narnia and would go on forever. The children were surprised at some of the creatures who loved Aslan; even people who had done some bad things were among them. Among this crowd were "friends . . . whom they had thought dead."

Like Narnia, Planet Earth will one day end, and then be replaced by "new heavens and new earth" that will never wear out; and like Narnia, this world must face Jesus before the new world begins. In the Gospel of Matthew, chapter 25, Jesus says, "When the Son of Man [Jesus] comes in his glory, and all the angels with him, he will sit on his throne in heavenly glory. All the nations will be gathered before him and he will separate the people one from another as a shepherd separates the sheep from the goats."

It is hard to imagine this world and everything in it ending; I do not know if it will be soon or a very long time from now. Even if it doesn't happen in our lifetimes, when we die, you and I will stand before

The End of the World

Jesus. This is what will matter then: that we loved Jesus and used our lives to express his love to others.

A prayer about seeing Aslan face to face:

> *Lord, I love this world and everything in it, yet I know you have an even better world prepared for the future. Help me to love Jesus and allow him to love others through me. I want to be able to look in his face with love and enter into that greater world forever.*

Meeting Aslan in the Next Life

In *The Last Battle*, we learn that people in Mr. Lewis's imaginary world serve two different gods; the Calormens worship Tash, a cruel and monstrous being, while the Narnians worship the great Lion Aslan.

Among the Calormene warriors, Emeth has an especially noble heart. He disagreed with his fellow soldiers when he learned they were treating the people of Narnia unfairly. When Emeth enters

Meeting Aslan in the Next Life

the magical door into Aslan's new world, he meets the great Lion. He falls down in terror and says to the Lion, "Alas, Lord, I am no son of Thine but the servant of Tash." Aslan answers Emeth and tells him, "Child, all the service thou hast done to Tash, I account as service done to me . . . unless thy desire had been for me thou wouldst not have sought so long and so truly. For all find what they seek."

The Bible, in chapter 25 of Matthew's Gospel, tells of a day when Jesus will invite those who loved him to enter into paradise: "For I was hungry and you gave me something to eat, I was thirsty and you gave me something to drink, I was a stranger and you invited me in, I needed clothes and you clothed me." Apparently, this blessing puzzles some people, who are like Emeth, and they say to Jesus, "Lord, when did we see you hungry and feed you, or thirsty and give you something to drink? When did we see you a stranger and invite you in, or needing clothes or clothe you?" He answers, "I tell you the truth, whatever you did for one the least of these brothers of mine, you did for me."

It is not always easy to understand what Mr. Lewis meant when he wrote something, and this talk between Emeth and Aslan confuses some readers of *The Last Battle*. Likewise, some Bible stories are easier to understand than others are, and the story of Jesus on the throne in Matthew 25 leaves some grown-up Bible readers scratching their heads. Who will be welcomed into Aslan's country, and who will

Following Aslan

Jesus invite to share his glory? Followers of Jesus do not always agree on how to answer these questions. One thing is clear, though: Jesus wants his followers to be kind to others. If we want to follow Jesus, we must show his love to everyone around us.

A prayer about meeting Aslan in the next life:

> *God, I know you loved the world, and that is why you sent your Son. Thank you that I can know and love him, so that I will be happy meeting him when I leave this life. Draw all those who seek truth to your Son, so that together we will be welcomed into your wonderful new world.*

The Real Narnia

At the end of *The Last Battle*, the land of Narnia ends, but the real Narnia begins at the same time. The creatures and humans of old Narnia follow Aslan through a magical door and find themselves in a beautiful new country. Shouting "Further up and further in," the crowd of humans and animals leap and laugh and run into this new land. They find it to be beautiful and strange, yet oddly familiar. Then they realize: it is Narnia—yet it is different from the old Narnia. They realize then that this is the real Narnia. Digory explains to Peter that the Narnia they knew "was only a shadow or a copy of the real Narnia, which has always been here . . . just as our own world . . . is only a shadow or a copy of something in Aslan's real world. . . . All of the old Narnia that mattered, all the dear creatures, have been drawn into the real Narnia." A few pages later, Lucy observes, "This is still Narnia, and more real and more beautiful than the Narnia down below."

When I was a little kid, I surprised my mother's minister one day by telling him that I did not want to go to heaven. He asked, "Why not?" and I told him, "It looks really boring, just sitting around all day playing harps on clouds. I don't like harp music, I don't like those silly white gowns they all wear, and I don't think it looks very exciting. I think I like my life on earth better than that." You see, all my ideas of heaven came from watching cartoons: in the cartoons when someone dies, they show up in heaven wearing white gowns and playing a harp on a cloud. The minister told me, "Don't worry: heaven is not like the cartoons—it will be a lot more exciting than that!"

The Bible doesn't really say much about heaven, but it does talk about a new Earth: "Then I saw a new heaven and a new earth, for the first heaven and the first earth had passed away" (Revelation 21:1).

The Real Narnia

We don't know details about the new Earth, but it sounds similar to this Earth in some ways: there is a city, the New Jerusalem, and the tree of life is there, and dead believers who have been resurrected. Resurrection does not mean people are like zombies or ghosts; instead, it means we will have new bodies like the ones we have now only better. Everything that is truly good in this world will continue in the next; only the sad and bad things will be missing. Most important, we will see Jesus face to face.

In the book of Romans, the Bible says that the entire creation—our whole world—is groaning and waiting to be made new. This will happen when Jesus returns and the world we live in today will end. There are so many beautiful, wonderful things to see on our Earth; but even if you could travel all over the world and see everything, this Earth isn't half as wonderful as the *real* Earth that is still to come!

A prayer about the real Earth:

> *God, you have made a wonderful world for us to live on. I love to see all the beauty, the creatures, and the people who share the Earth with me. But I know you have something even better in store for us—a new Earth, the real Earth, even more spectacular than this one. Thank you that you will heal this old Earth, so that nothing good will be lost. I can't wait to be with you forever.*

The Great Story That Goes on Forever

I always cry when I read the very end of *The Last Battle*, the final pages of all *The Chronicles of Narnia*. I've read it at least a half dozen times, and I still get teary-eyed, not because I'm sad, but because it makes me feel so joyful and hopeful.

At the end of the story, all the characters from all the Narnia books are reunited. Lucy, Edmund, Susan, and Peter; Digory and Polly; Caspian and Mr. Tumnus and of course Reepicheep the noble mouse all are together in the real Narnia. They

The Great Story That Goes on Forever

walk together, "a great, bright procession" up "mountains higher than you could see in this world . . . forests and green slopes and sweet orchards and flashing waterfalls, one above the other, going up forever." Of course, most important of all, Aslan is forever with them.

Mr. Lewis finishes the story like this: "The things that began to happen after that were so great and beautiful that I cannot write them . . . for us this is the end of all the stories. . . . But for them it was the only the beginning of the real story . . . now at last they were beginning Chapter One of the Great Story, which no one on earth has read: which goes on forever: in which every chapter is better than the one before."

You are still very young, and you are so full of life that you probably don't think much about your life ending: for that matter, it seems even crazier at your age to think of the whole world ending! However, someday this life will end for you, one way or another. You don't need to feel scared or sad, though, because the end of your life on Earth will not be a real ending. For those who follow Aslan—or Jesus—there are no endings, only beginnings. You will enter into a new story, one that no one on this Earth has ever read, where "every chapter is better than the one before."

Following Aslan

A prayer about endings and beginnings:

> *God, the Bible says you are Alpha and Omega (the A and the Z), the beginning of everything and the end. You sent Jesus to lead me through life on this earth, and when that story has ended, he will lead me into an even greater and unending adventure. Thank you that I can be with Jesus forever.*

About the Author

Kenneth McIntosh lives in Flagstaff, Arizona, with his wife, Marsha, and a small menagerie of pets. They have two college-age children, Jonathan and Eirené. Ken writes, teaches, and serves as pastor for The Journey (a church he founded). He enjoys hiking, watching movies, learning about other cultures, and driving his vintage Volkswagen. The works of C. S. Lewis, especially *The Chronicles of Narnia, The Great Divorce,* and *Mere Christianity,* have nurtured Ken in the course of his spiritual journey. He says it is his lifelong goal to follow Aslan.

About the Illustrators

Evangeline Ehl graduated with honors from Pensacola Christian College with a degree in commercial art. By day she works as an award-winning graphic designer but moonlights in portraiture and various types of illustration. As a versatile fine artist, she illustrates both in digital and traditional media. Evangeline and her husband live in West Texas. Her free time is spent chasing down her two Dobermans, Kaiser and Tara.

MK Bassett-Harvey is an award-winning graphic designer and illustrator. Her interests include wildlife illustration and landscape painting. She currently lives in upstate New York with her husband, Chuck, and children, Noël and Jeffrey.

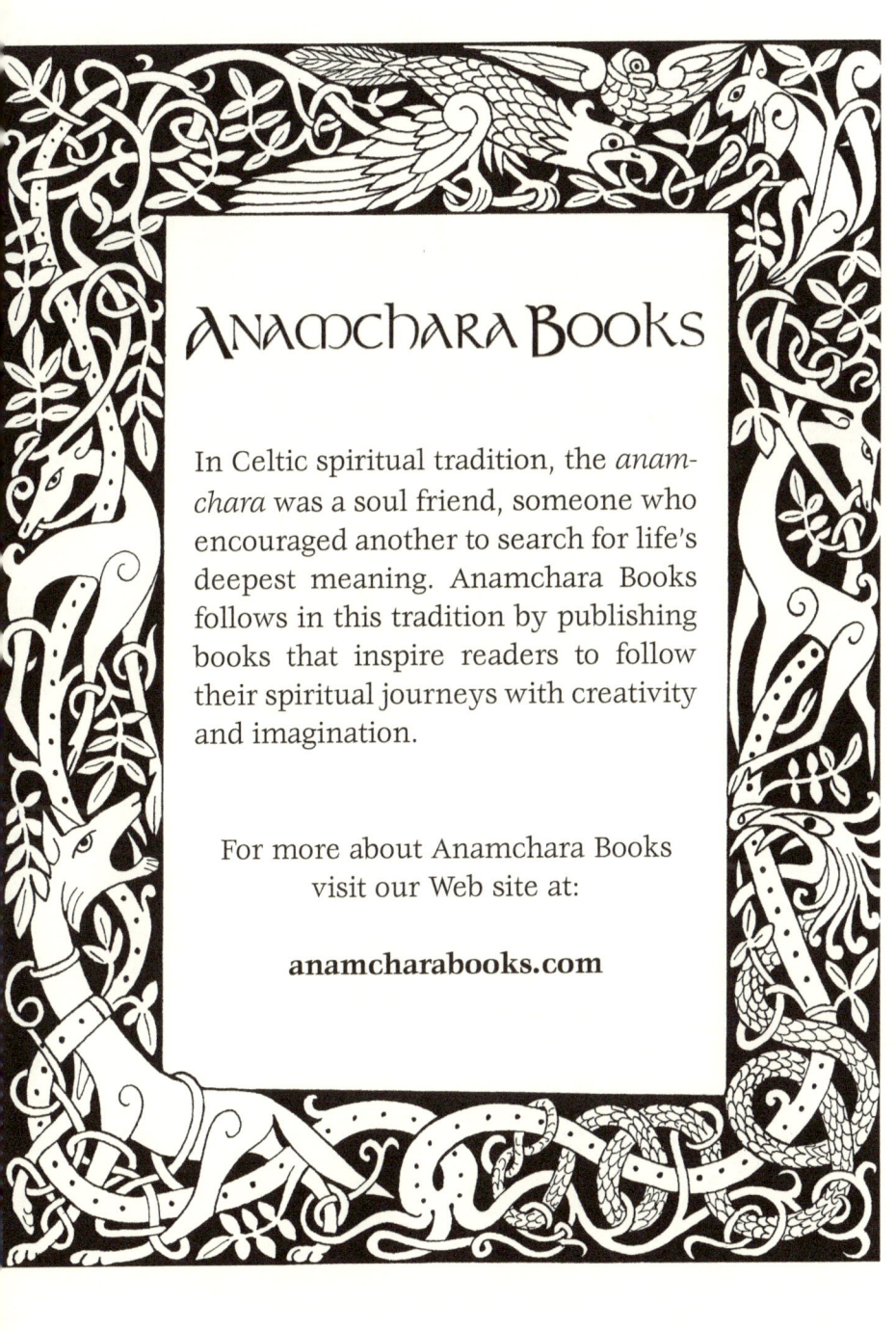

Anamchara Books

In Celtic spiritual tradition, the *anamchara* was a soul friend, someone who encouraged another to search for life's deepest meaning. Anamchara Books follows in this tradition by publishing books that inspire readers to follow their spiritual journeys with creativity and imagination.

For more about Anamchara Books visit our Web site at:

anamcharabooks.com